Contents

What is a school?

A school is a place where you go to learn.

Children go to school to learn together. These children go to The Grove Infant School. Every day, their teacher greets them at the classroom door.

All the classes in Grove School are named after trees. These children are in Ash Class. They made this **logo** for the classroom door.

by Charlie

AT YOUR SCHOOL
Design a logo for your classroom door.

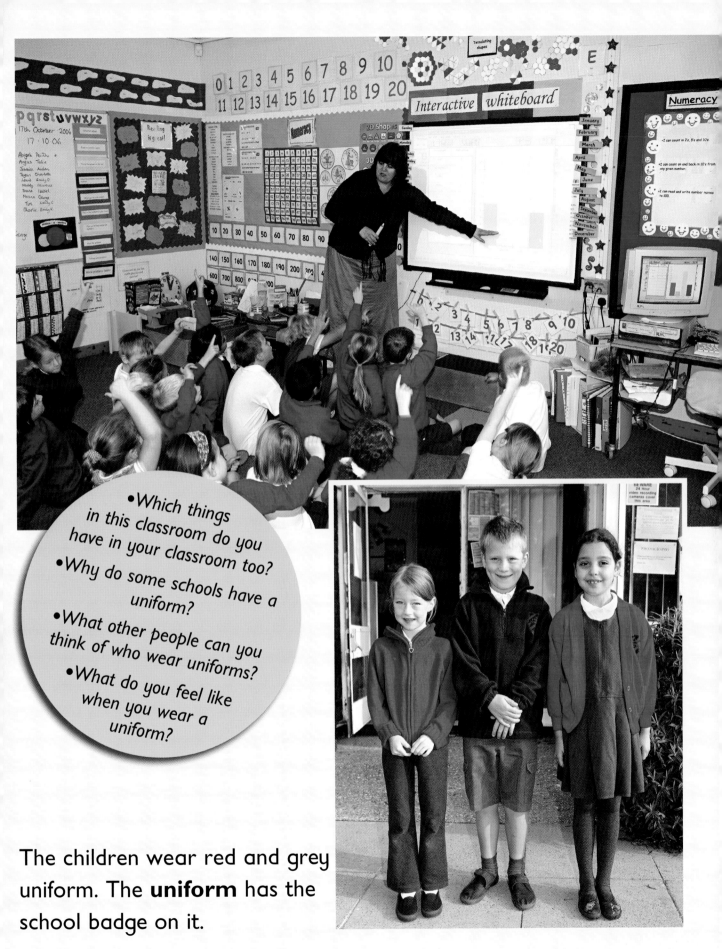

- Which things in this classroom do you have in your classroom too?
- Why do some schools have a uniform?
- What other people can you think of who wear uniforms?
- What do you feel like when you wear a uniform?

The children wear red and grey uniform. The **uniform** has the school badge on it.

Different types of schools

All schools are different. Some schools have hundreds of children and some are much smaller.

AT YOUR SCHOOL
With your class, plan to make a book called 'Around Our School'.

Grove School is quite a new school, but the school above is much older.

•How old is your school building?
•How many children go to your school?
•What is your school's name?

•What does your school have to help children or other people who use a wheelchair?

•Does your school have special things for children who need help to see, hear or speak?

This picture shows a special school for children who have **disabilities**. The boy needs help to speak. He is learning to use a **voice pad**.

Some schools are mainly for children from one **religion**. These children go to an Islamic school.

9

What's in a classroom?

A classroom needs a place for the children to leave their belongings.

It needs tables, chairs, books and computers.

- Where do you keep your things at school?
- Which things in your classroom need electricity to work?

Ash Class made these rules for their classroom.

Golden Rules
- Don't push people.
- Help each other.
- Be polite.
- Always wash your hands after going to the toilet and before eating.
- Be kind to each other.
- Respect each other.
- Always listen to each other and the teacher.
- Always help each other to tidy up.
- Always tuck your chairs in.
- Work quietly at your table.

A classroom needs space on the walls to display the children's work and somewhere to wash brushes after painting.

- What is on the walls in your classroom?
- Which of Ash Class's rules do you think is the most important? Why?

AT YOUR SCHOOL
Make a **plan** of your classroom. Put in as much detail as you can.

The school grounds

At many schools, the children walk through a gate into the school grounds.

Ash Class go through the gate and along a path by the side of the playing field.

At the end of the path they come to the playground and the main school building.

- Why do schools have a school gate?
- Which types of trees and other plants are in your school grounds?
- What games do children play in the playground?

There are things painted on the playground, including a **compass** (below).

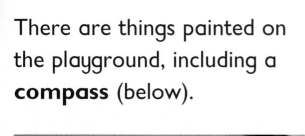

This is a photograph of the school, looking down from the air. It is called an **aerial view**.

You can see the school building and the playground and trees in front of it.

- What do the letters stand for on the compass?
- What game are the girls playing?

AT YOUR SCHOOL
Find out if you live north, south, east or west of your school.

13

The school building

A school building is made up of different types of rooms. As well as classrooms, there is a hall. In the hall, all the children and their teachers can meet together.

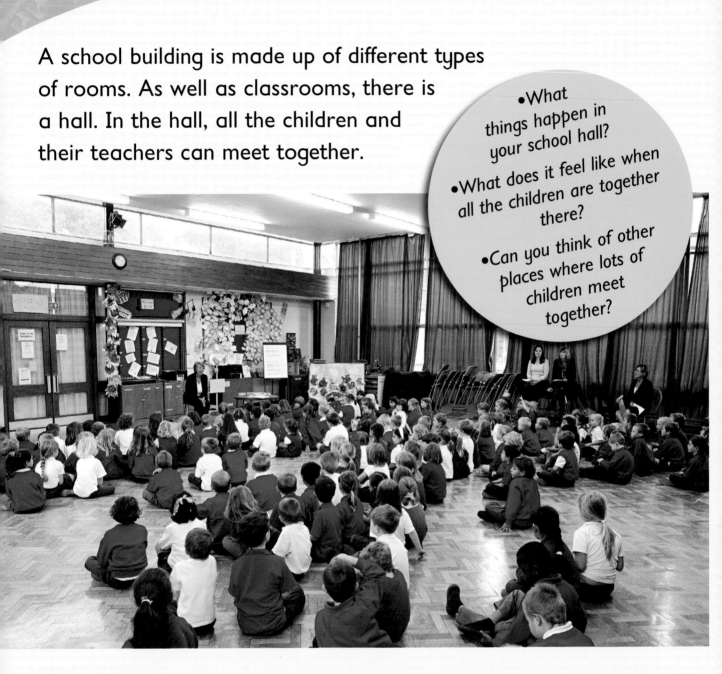

- What things happen in your school hall?
- What does it feel like when all the children are together there?
- Can you think of other places where lots of children meet together?

AT YOUR SCHOOL
Make a large plan of your school building and the grounds. Include all the rooms, doors and corridors. Draw on footsteps to show the way from the school gate to your classroom.

Other types of room in
a school include:
- the library
- the kitchen
- the dining room
- the **staffroom**
- the **office**.

- What does 'Welcome' mean?
- What makes you feel welcome in a place?
- Who is the staffroom for?
- Does your school have a garden?

Grove School
has a garden
in the middle.
Some rooms
have windows
that look out
to the garden.

The head teacher and secretary

Lots of different people work at a school.

The head teacher is in charge of everything that happens there. She welcomes visitors and talks to them about the school.

Welcome to
The Grove Infant & Nursery School

HEADTEACHER:
Mrs. S.A.Bird

CARETAKERS:
Mr.E.Neville
Mrs.M.Neville

The teachers at Grove School tell the head teacher how the children are doing. She gives badges for good behaviour.

- What is your head teacher called?
- How many other teachers work at your school?
- What type of things do you think the children at this school do to receive a 'good behaviour badge'?

The **secretary** has an office next to the head teacher's office.

AT YOUR SCHOOL
Think of questions to ask your school secretary about his or her work.

- What is your school secretary called?
- When does your teacher mark your class register?
- Why is it important to know which children are in the school each day?

The secretary types letters and answers the telephone.

She keeps a record of where the children live and of any special things they need.

Each day children take their class **register** to the secretary, so that she knows who is in the school.

17

Other staff

Everyone who works at the school tries to make sure that the children are safe and happy.

The **caretaker** looks after the school buildings and grounds.

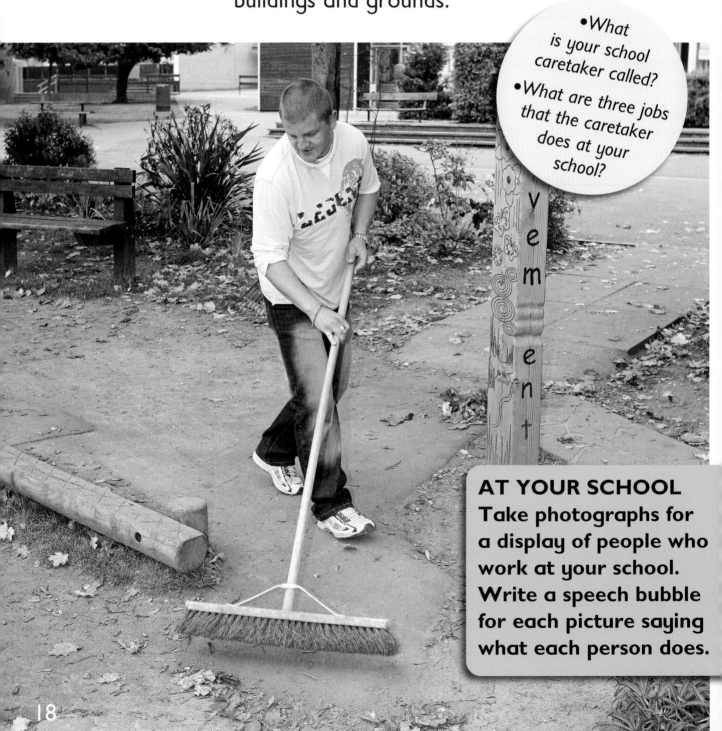

• What is your school caretaker called?
• What are three jobs that the caretaker does at your school?

AT YOUR SCHOOL
Take photographs for a display of people who work at your school. Write a speech bubble for each picture saying what each person does.

Workers in the kitchen prepare and serve food for the children's lunch.

Dinner ladies (below) make sure that the children take their turn to go in for lunch.

- What uniform do the cooks and dinner ladies wear at your school?
- Why do the cooks wear hats?
- What problems sometimes happen in the playground?

At playtime, helpers (right) are there to solve problems. Many helpers are parents, who work at the school as **volunteers**.

How do you get to school?

In your class, you could make a block graph to show how many children travel to school:

- by car
- by walking
- by bus
- by train
- by bike
- by any other means.

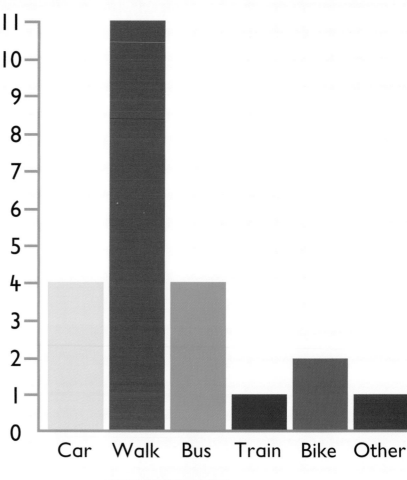

- How many children in your class cycle to school?
- Which is your favourite way to get to school?
- How far is it from your home to your school?
- What road signs and road markings are outside your school?

School Safety Zone

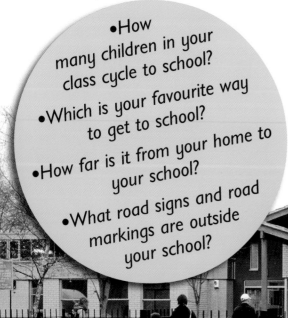

These children walk to school as part of a walking bus.

•Why do people in a walking bus wear yellow jackets?
•Why do you think it is called a walking bus?
•Does your school do something special in 'Walk to School Month'?
• Why do people think it is good to walk to school?

The walking bus follows the same route every day. It waits at places along the route, at certain times, so that more children can join it.

AT YOUR SCHOOL
On your way to school, look around and try to spot changes that are taking place – for example, to buildings or to fields and trees. You will see more if you walk!

International Walk to School month
walktoschool.org.uk

Your school address

Your school is in a street, and the street is in a village or town.

You can find the street on a **street map** of your village or town.

- What is the name of the street where your school is?
- Where does the street lead to?
- On a street map, what symbols are used for a church and for a railway station?
- What is the name of your town or village?
- Which other towns do you travel to?

You can find your town or village on a **road map**. The road map shows how your town or village is linked to other places.

Remember to look at the **key**, to find out what **symbols** on the map mean.

If you wanted to send a letter to Ash Class, you would write their name and **address** in lines like this.

This is the town

This is the **county**

This is the post code

Ash Class,
The Grove Infant School,
Dark Lane,
Harpenden,
Hertfordshire,
AL5 1QD

The post code helps postmen and women to sort your letters.

AT YOUR SCHOOL
Write and send a letter or card. Write the address properly!

23

Where in the world?

Grove School is in the south-east of England, quite near to London.

England is one part of the country called the United Kingdom (the UK). The other parts of the UK are Scotland, Wales and Northern Ireland.

Can you find the UK on a globe?

- Which part of the UK do you live in?
- Do you live in the north, south, east or west of the country?
- Do you live in a large town or city or in a village?

AT YOUR SCHOOL
Describe your town or village, and where it is, for someone who lives in another country.

The UK belongs to the **continent** of Europe. Far away, on the continent of Asia, is a country called Sri Lanka. The people there are trying to build new schools, after many villages and towns were destroyed by a **tsunami**.

Ash Class and other classes at Grove School collect boxes of books, crayons and other things to give to a new school in Sri Lanka (right). People from the UK take the boxes to the school (below).

- Can you find Sri Lanka on a globe?
- What would you give to the 'Classroom in a Box'?
- Does your school have links with other countries in the world?

25

Schools in the past

You could find out about the history of your school.

- How old is the school?
- What was there before it was built?
- Did the school once have a different building, in a different place?
- Are there pictures of the school in the past?

•What is the police officer teaching the children about in the picture below?

•What else is happening in the pretend street?

•Do visitors come to talk to the children at your school? Who do you remember?

Here is a picture from about 80 years ago. A police officer went to the school to tell the children about road safety. He made a pretend street in the school hall.

This picture shows a teacher and her class in the year 1919.

•What differences are there between this classroom and yours?
•What similarities are there?
•What do you think it would be like going to school in 1912?

WHERE YOU LIVE
Look for Victorian school buildings. Some are still schools. Some have been changed into homes, offices, libraries or other public buildings.

This school was built in **Victorian** times. In those days there were separate parts of the school for boys and girls over the age of 7. Today all the classes have girls and boys.

Glossary

Address The exact place where someone's home or another building is. An address includes the number or name of the building, the street name, the town name, and a post code.

Aerial view A picture or photograph of something, seen from above.

Caretaker A person who is in charge of looking after a building and, often, its grounds as well.

Compass A picture that shows the direction of North, South, East and West. A compass is also an instrument used by travellers. It has a needle which always points towards North.

Continent A very large area of the world's land, such as Europe, Africa, Asia and North America.

County An area of the UK.

Disabilities Difficulties with some part of everyday living, such as moving, seeing, hearing or learning. The difficulties may be caused by an illness or an accident.

Key A list of the symbols used on a map and what each symbol means.

Logo A small picture or pattern, used as a symbol.

Office A place where business is done. Office work includes writing, keeping records and organising things.

Plan A simple type of map, showing the shapes you would see if you looked down on a place from above.

Register A book in which a record is kept every day of who is at school.

Religion A set of beliefs and special things that are done by people who hold those beliefs. People in the UK belong to the Christian, Muslim, Jewish, Hindu, Sikh and Buddhist religions.

Road map A map that shows how to travel by road from one village or town to another. The map does not show all the streets that make up a village or town.

Secretary A person who types, deals with letters and phone calls, and does other office work for a person or an organisation.

Staffroom A room for the staff, which means all the teachers at a school.

Street map A large-scale map that shows all the streets in a place. It also includes particular buildings and parks, etc, that people may need to find.

Symbols Very simple pictures, letters or colours that are used to represent particular things. For example, on a street map, PO represents a post office.

Tsunami An enormous wave in the sea, which travels very fast. It is usually caused by an earthquake or volcano under the sea.

Uniform Clothing that shows that the wearer belongs to a certain group of people.

Victorian From the time of Queen Victoria. She was queen of Great Britain from 1837 to 1901.

Voice pad A machine that helps people who have a speech disability.

Volunteers People who work for no pay, because they like to help an organisation.

Further information

Some schools have websites that tell you all about their buildings, people and activities.

http://www.topmarks.co.uk/Default.aspx links you to some schools with especially good websites.

http://www.woodlands-junior.kent.sch.uk /customs/topics/index.htm has lots of useful information for projects about Britain. You can look up a topic, such as Schools, in the long A to Z list.

You can visit a Victorian school on the internet, at

http://www.taw.org.uk/LIC/BH3/ VictorianSchool.htm

To find a street map for where you live, type in your post code at

http://www.streetmap.co.uk/

http://mapzone.ordnancesurvey.co.uk/ is a free site that aims to teach you mapping skills in a fun way.

To find out about the Walk to School campaign, go to

http://www.walktoschool.org.uk/

There are some museums that show you what schools were like in the past. Sometimes you can dress up as a child in Victorian times and have a lesson from those days. These museums include:

British Schools Museum, Hitchin
   http://www.btinternet.com/~skua/school/

Radstock Museum, Radstock, Bath
   http://www.radstockmuseum.co.uk/

Ragged School Museum, London
   http://www.raggedschoolmuseum.org.uk/

Scotland Street School Museum, Glasgow
   http://www.glasgowmuseums.com/ven ue/index.cfm?venueid=12

Books

Family Scrapbook: School Life in the 1940s and 50s, Faye Gardner, 2005 (Evans Publishing)

Going for a Walk: Around a School, Sally Hewitt, 2005 (Franklin Watts)

Growing Up in World War Two: School, Catherine Burch, 2005 (Franklin Watts)

One World: Going to School, Amanda Rayner, 2007 (Franklin Watts)

People Who Help Us: Teacher, Rebecca Hunter, 2005 (Evans Publishing)

Start-Up Geography: Journey to School, Anna Lee, 2004 (Evans Publishing)

Taking Part: A Caring School, Sally Hewitt, 2006 (Franklin Watts)

Taking Part: An Eco School, Sally Hewitt, 2006 (Franklin Watts)

Why Manners Matter: At School, Jillian Powell, 2005 (Franklin Watts)

Index